Creative RE

GW01255417

Introduction

Damien Hirst's recent art work is a human skull (a real one) encrusted with over £12 million worth of diamonds. The work is entitled 'For the love of God' (partly, at least, because that is what Damien's mum said when he told her what he was making). As with so much of his work, the objects he creates reflect his interest in life, death, wealth, ambiguity and the search for meaning. It sold for £50 million.

That's rather like RE (except Hirst makes 2000 times your salary). The connections between art and religions are variously described, but the relationship has never been simple. Sometimes religion attacks art (as the iconoclasts did), but sometimes art attacks religion (those stupid Danish cartoons of the Prophet spring to mind). Sometimes religion uses art instrumentally (lots of kitschy objects associated with the Sacred Heart of Jesus), but sometimes it's the other way round (I'm thinking of Madonna's video for 'Like a Prayer', which appropriated the imagery of the crucifixion to sell her records).

This book is not just concerned with visual art, though. We have sought here to provide some well-worked teaching ideas for the RE classroom that use the arts from within religions to raise questions of meaning and purpose. And we have also tried to be alert to the creativity of pupils. If RE is to set the highest possible standards of learning, a part of its task is to unlock and liberate imaginative and creative talent in pursuit of the spirituality that makes meaning in life. This can be done by any child.

This short book provides ideas that refer to many religions, and might apply to every pupil. We hope teachers will find ideas here that they would like to try, and the confidence that comes from such ideas being presented in 'classroom ready' ways. Even better, your own adaptations of these ideas add your creativity as a teacher to the starting points we offer.

Whether it is through architecture, music, art, poetry or playdough, good teaching in RE benefits from creativity

Lat Blaylock

Series Editor

Contents

Creative RE: frequently asked questions

1. What is creativity?

One definition of creativity is that it's about 'imaginative activity fashioned so as to produce outcomes that are both original and of value'. Professor Ken Robinson's influential 1999 report *All Our Futures* identifies creativity as: 'something diverse and multifaceted; possible in all fields of human intelligence, not just the arts; existing in all people in one form or another. The creative processes are developed through practical application and in all subject areas. They require pupils to learn control, techniques, knowledge, skills, understanding as well as having the freedom and confidence to experiment'. This raises the question: is RE a creative subject? Sometimes it is. This book is designed to help you, the teacher, realise the potential for creative excellence in RE.

2. Why should RE be creative?

There are at least four areas in which this question can be answered.

- First, RE should be creative because many (all?) pupils have creative abilities and talents. Many pupils prefer, and do better when using the creative intelligences than when approaching RE merely through factual learning. Using these aptitudes for better RE is an obvious route to better motivation and higher standards.

- Secondly, RE should be creative because religions are creative. Every religion has phases of dynamic and stimulating creativity. When religions begin, when they reform, and when they inspire, it is often a creative process.

- Thirdly, RE should be creative because teachers enjoy their work more if it is. None of us really believes that RE has been good if all that has happened is that we've transmitted 400 facts from inside our heads to the inside of the pupils' heads. One way or another, creativity is part of good RE. If our pupils are more creative than we are, then we learn from them.

- Finally, I suggest religions and human beings need to make – create – meaning. If your lifetime is the raw material out of which you make the meaning of life, then RE gives pupils some tools and guidance about how to do this. Making up the meaning of life is a creative process. Philosophy and religion have in common their intention to make meaning out of experience. RE can help any child to do this creatively.

3. What's creative about religion?

Religions often exalt the divine creativity, and see human creativity as exalted. For many believers, God is a maker and humanity shows an imprint of the divine when we make, create, imagine, dream, sing, compose or dance. This takes many forms, of course – aesthetic diversity is normal within religions – but word, image, symbol, vision, design and song often energise spiritual life within religions, and beyond them all. Plainsong, Zen Gardens and Sufi silence are almost the opposite of an Orthodox iconostasis, the complexities of mosque decoration, or the splendours of the Hindu murti. Still, making space sacred and making time holy are creative activities in all faiths.

4. I can't draw, and I have no taps in my classroom: shall I throw this book away?

No. What a creative teacher creates might be opportunities for learning rather than lino cuts, oil paintings or musical scores. It's certainly the case that teachers can enable the art and music of their pupils without being able to make art or music themselves. The practical issues for RE are sharp: curriculum time is short, and facilities and materials often non-existent. Still (as we hope the book shows) creativity can happen in five minutes of thinking, or with a pencil and paper. You don't have to build a juggernaut carnival float in 25 lessons each week.

5. Are all pupils creative?

It's important to remember that there are pupils whose terror at being asked to draw or be dramatic is deep and real. Not every pupil can be creative in any particular art form. Still, where a more personalised curriculum is being planned in RE, it is wise to ask: how will the creativity of each pupil be engaged? Words and music, pictures and the internet can all be foci for creative spiritual explorations. It's also interesting to link creativity to spirituality. Where spiritual development is promoted by learning in RE, then responses to this are often creative and imaginative. Is it perhaps true that if you have a pupil who is totally uncreative, the school should seek to spark off a change in that young person?

6. How can I enable creative thinking among my pupils in RE?

Thinking creatively happens where ideas are fresh, or are combined in unexpected ways. Juxtapositions of the unusual or new angles on old thoughts make for ideas and approaches that are bold and take risks. In the annual NATRE 'Art in Heaven' competition, we are always challenged by the thinking about God which pupils produce. Recent entries have suggested that God is like a security camera, a search engine, a black hole, a hair shirt and a rainbow butterfly. (Do you see why? See the results at www.natre.org.uk/spiritedarts.) A key focus in this book is to offer activities for the classroom that open up the possibility of fresh thinking. Many teachers report that they and their pupils really enjoy creative RE activities, learning a lot. We hope you find some here that work for you.

7. Can creativity make for high standards in RE?

The worst kind of RE lacks challenge. At first, pupils think it is a 'nice doss' to colour the Sea of Galilee blue. Actually, it's a waste of precious RE time, and it's not creative. There is of course a tension between covering curriculum content effectively and setting up lessons with time enough for imagination to flourish. The best solution to this is to manage the tension, because teachers know that creative work is often the best, most rigorous, that pupils do. Another issue is about assessing RE that is creative. 'Isn't that just subjective?' teachers ask. We have taken the view in this book that the eight-level scale does make space for progression and rigour in creative learning. See how various articles use 'I can…' statements to clarify what has been achieved through applied imagination. In planning and creating this book, we have tried to offer demanding ways of being creative in RE. Every teacher will have some of their own too.

8.   Where can I find supporting resources for creative RE?

Here are some starting points from government sources

Creativity: find it, promote it

This site provides detailed information on approaches to the creativity dimension, including whole-school guidance and subject-specific examples. www.ncaction.org.uk/creativity/

All our futures: creativity, culture and education

In this report, the National Advisory Committee on Creative and Cultural Education puts forward the case for developing creative and cultural education. It considers what is involved, looks at current provision, and assesses the opportunities and obstacles. www.dcsf.gov.uk/naccce/

Creative partnerships

Creative Partnerships enable schools to work with creative practitioners to develop a broad, balanced and relevant curriculum. It enables practitioners to work in partnership with schools, developing long-term, sustainable relationships. It is very encouraging that there are about 50 case studies relevant to RE on this site. www.creative-partnerships.com/

Nurturing creativity in young people: five hours a week

Following a review of creativity in schools in 2006, *Nurturing Creativity in Young People* was published jointly by the Department of Culture, Media and Sport and the DCFS. This report provided a framework for creativity, starting with early years, developing through primary and secondary education and leading to pathways in the creative industries. This is the report that has led to the Government's stated intention of providing five hours of creative, cultural and sporting activity each week through school. Find the report at www.culture.gov.uk/reference_library.

9.   Where shall I start? Summarising creative RE

- Any teacher, any pupil, can be more creative in learning.

- Religions are creative meaning-making systems. Good RE is similar.

- Use RE objectives to drive planning – it's the link to religion and spirituality that drives the learning in RE. Syllabus links matter and they are not hard to find, as religions are often creative.

- Modelling matters – use the excellence of other pupils' creative work to inspire your pupils.

- Remember that creative learning may not map onto other measures of ability: some pupils excel in a creative lesson, but don't shine in an argument. Their talents are to be nurtured.

- Creative thinking is a key need in RE for the coming years, motivating and energising engagement for teachers and many learners.

- Creative writing deserves more space in RE, where poetry, liturgy, parable, creed and fiction can express spiritual depth for pupils.

- Spiritual energy and creative energy seem very close to each other. Both can drive good RE.

- You're a creative teacher – but some of your pupils may be more creative than you in some ways!

- Great creative education in RE is not discipline free, so you have to work at it.

Creativity and RE: the issues

Religions are creative: RE does well to approach religions through the things they create. These include art, architecture, music, texts, poems, dramas. Creative RE is not only about pupils being creative. They don't always have to make things!

Creative learners: Pupils have many talents and skills in being creative and imaginative. RE needs to use and develop these abilities. This is about learning styles, space, time and opportunities. What moves pupils from timidity through confidence to maturity in creativity?

Creativity and ICT: What are the new potentialities for creative RE through ICT? How can teachers see, use and develop the potential creativity of ICT into actuality? Collaborative creativity – between subjects, or groups of pupils – is needed for films, podcasts, and blogging.

Creative teachers: If you want creative learning, you'll need creative teachers. What helps? How can this help be shared out? Every teacher is creative in some ways.

RE has frontiers with expressive arts: poetry, dance, drama, art, sculpture, music. Should these be more of a focus for development than our other frontiers with history and geography?

Creativity and RE: the issues

Creative planning: How can teachers escape the feelings of dread and dullness that lead to weak and uninspired planning? Planned creativity could feel false, but preparing for it is important.

Making meaning: Creativity and philosophical RE – religions make meaning. Being human involves making meaning out of experience. So creativity in RE is about life's quest for meaning purpose and truth – even more than about paint and playdough.

Framework and structures: Syllabuses, frameworks and exam specifications could stifle creativity, but some teachers use them to set imagination loose. Creativity leads through discipline to satisfaction, and the discipline of planning can help.

'Be creative' feels threatening:

'I'm not arty.'

'I'm dealing with too much content to be creative.'

'I haven't time.'

'We have no taps.'

Answers? This book offers some, but we have no grants for taps.

Creative thinking: Using thinking skills on RE topics makes learning more creative. Whether it is Edward de Bono's six hats, lateral thinking or Philosophy for Children, get them to craft or manufacture new ideas. What makes pupils creative in their thoughts? Set that up for RE.

Music with meaning: exploring and expressing spirituality and beliefs through music and lyrics

For the teacher

Music can be a valuable way to enhance pupils' spiritual awareness and to encourage personal reflection and expression of insight and meaning. Music is a universal language that is instinctively understood by all. In RE it can provide 'a window' into the beliefs and values of others and act as a stimulus for discussion.

Music can play an important part in our lives. It can

- uplift the spirits

- stimulate reflection

- educate

- connect with significant moments in life – events which give a sense of identity, value or purpose

- be evocative and subtle, or literal.

Music can convey very powerful messages about life, death, meaning and value. Some musicians use their songs to put across their beliefs and ideas, in the hope that listeners will share their concerns. The following classroom activities use music from contemporary culture, Islam and Christianity as a stimulus for

- exploring spiritual ideas and religious beliefs

- encouraging pupils to express their own spiritual and religious insights creatively through music and lyrics.

' ... listening to Bob Marley taught me as much about religion, culture, and politics as I learnt in church and in RE in school. It gave me an alternative story – a story that I could buy in to.'

Dr Robert Beckford (Reader in Black Theology and Culture at Oxford Brookes University and author of a number of books in the field of religion, popular culture and politics)

For information: music and Islam

Some Muslims question whether music is compatible with the teachings of the Qur'an. Some believe that string and wind instruments are haram (unlawful or forbidden), but for many Muslims percussion is acceptable. The Nasheed tradition uses the sound of the human voice alone. Some Muslims today, such as Yusuf Islam and Sami Yusuf, recognise how music is a powerful way of communicating understanding of Muslim beliefs and values in the Western world.

> Islamic Art, whether in the form of calligraphy, tiles, or music is all inspired by divine love and beauty.
>
> Sami Yusuf

Expectations and outcomes

If a pupil is able to say yes to some of these then they are working at:

I can....

Level 4

- use religious vocabulary to **describe** a message of a piece of music written by a religious believer and **explain** why that person wrote it

- **describe** something I find spiritual and inspiring in the lyrics of a song or in a piece of music, **applying** spiritual ideas for myself.

Level 5

- **explain** the possible **impact** of listening to particular pieces of religious music on (i) a non-believer's life (ii) a believer's life

- **explain** or express, using appropriate media, what I find uplifting or inspiring, or provoking of serious thought or contemplation, in some music I love.

Activity 1 A starter

Aim: to explore how music can express inner feelings and beliefs

Method

- Break the class into small groups of 4–5 students.

- Play several different types of music which express spiritual or religious feelings. (You can use both contemporary and classical.) Some suggestions can be found below – but get your students to suggest others.

- Following each piece of music, ask the groups to share ideas about how the person who wrote the music or lyrics might have been feeling when they wrote it. Focus questions could be:

  o How does it make you feel?

  o Do you think it makes others feel the same way?

  o What does the music/lyric tell you about the person who composed it?

  o Which lyric or section conveys the message of the music most strongly?

- Feed back ideas and note responses on a board.

- Hold a group discussion about how music is used in society today and, in particular, in religions.

- Ask pupils to brainstorm some ways in which music is used to express spiritual feelings and beliefs today. For example music is used for…

  o praise, thanksgiving

  o reflection or meditation

  o articulating important beliefs/values principles

  o celebration – e.g. festivals, weddings

  o intercession – prayer.

- List any genres of religious music they know, for example:

  o hymns/praise songs

  o kirtan – the musical recitation of hymns from Guru Granth Sahib in Sikhism

  o nasheeds – spiritual songs in Islam

  o spirituals

  o classical pieces e.g. Handel's Messiah.

Resources

CDs, player, flipchart paper and pens

Music suggestions to get you started:

Contemporary culture

Black Eyed Peas	'Where is the love?'
Bob Marley	'War'
U2	'Pride'
James Blunt	'Cry'
Yusuf Islam	'One Day at a Time' (*An Other Cup* album 2006)

Worship / spiritual music

Taize music – spiritual, reflective, prayerful – MP3 files for download from http://www.taize.fr/en_article681.html

Islamic Nasheed

Towards the Light album by Zain Bhikha available from the RE Today catalogue

Dawud Wharnsby Ali – e.g 'Salam – A Piece of Peace', *Enter into Peace* album. Lyrics available on http://www.wharnsby.com/Lyrics/index.html

Yusuf Islam http://www.mountainoflight.co.uk/

Click videos to find link to a short portrait of Yusuf's life in music (links to YouTube video: Profile of a Performing Artist Yusuf (Cat Stevens))

See also: http://www.catstevens.com/

Activity 2 Exploring how music conveys powerful messages

A Muslim response to acts of terrorism

Sami Yusuf, a young British Muslim who has become 'Islam's biggest rock star' (*Time Magazine*), uses music and lyrics to convey the real face of Islam as understood by the majority of Muslims – one of peace and tolerance. He does not shy away from tackling controversial themes in his lyrics and videos. He has criticised Muslim rebels from Chechnya for the Beslan massacre, and the French government for banning headscarves in schools, as well as singing out about the oppression of Muslims in Palestine and Lebanon.

Muhammad (pbuh)

(Dedicated to the innocent children of Beslan)

Every day I see the same headlines

Crimes committed in the name of the divine

People committing atrocities in his name

They murder and kidnap with no shame

But did he teach hatred, violence, or bloodshed? No... Oh No

He taught us about human brotherhood

And against prejudice he firmly stood

He loved children, their hands he'd hold

And taught his followers to respect the old

So would he allow the murder of an innocent child? Oh No...

CHORUS:

Muhammad ya rasulallah

Muhammad ya habiballah

Muhammad ya khalilallah

Muhammad

Muhammad ya rasulallah

Muhammad ya shafi'allah

Muhammad ya bashirallah

Ya rasulallah

Muhammad the light of my eyes

About you they spread many lies

If only they came to realise

Bloodshed you despise

CHORUS

Lyrics: Sami Yusuf & Bara Kherigi   Composition: Sami Yusuf

> CHORUS: (English translation) Muhammad oh Prophet of God
>
> Muhammad oh beloved of God
>
> Muhammad oh Friend of God Muhammad
>
> Muhammad oh prophet of God
>
> Muhammad oh interceder (on behalf of humanity)
>
> Muhammad oh good news Oh Prophet of God

Sami Yusuf
© Awakening worldwide 2002-2006
To find out more about Sami Yusuf visit http://www.samiyusuf.com/home/index.htm

For the teacher

Music, carefully used, is a great way of encouraging the skills of reflection and response. In this example the pupils may need a reminder of the events of Beslan.

Reflecting

It provides time and space to pupils to listen, think, imagine and reflect. It is often good to provide a lyric sheet, or invite pupils to draw as they listen, or focus on something visual as well as listening.

Expressing

Conversation and discussion:

- What did you think Sami Yusuf was feeling about the world today when he wrote this song?

- What is the main message of the song? What are your thoughts about this?

- What does the song tell us about the teachings and example of Muhammad? Why do you think Sami feels this is so important for people to understand today? Why might music be a good way of communicating this?

Responding

Poetry / song lyrics / artwork

- Choose one key idea or line from the song and express your own thoughts about it in a poem, lyrics or through collage or poster work.

Used with permission
This song can be found on *My Ummah*, Sami Yusuf. © 2005 Awakening: www.awakening.org

Activity 3 Compare and contrast

Listen to music from contemporary culture with a similar theme to the message of Sami Yusuf. A good example is the track: Where is the Love?' by the Black Eyed Peas

- Play the song.

- Display a copy of the lyrics on the IWB – you can find them on www.lyrics007.com.

- Ask pupils to highlight the phrases which sum up the main message of the song.

- How is this similar to the message of Sami Yusuf? (Answers will include children being hurt; the issue of suffering in the world; the need for people to 'practise what is preached' – to follow the true message of love and peace, not a distorted message from a minority with particular political objectives.)

- In what ways is it different? (Sami is speaking about Muhammad (Prophet of God). Black Eyed Peas are calling upon God (Father) to help us and to provide 'guidance from above'.)

- The Black Eyed Peas sum up the problems in the world with the Question 'Where is the Love?' Can you suggest a key question to sum up the message found in the Sami Yusuf song?

- In pairs/as a class brainstorm other contemporary songs which convey a Christian or a Muslim message. If possible play a range of these in class and identify the 'powerful' messages they contain.

- Create some lyrics, a piece of music, an image (e.g. a CD cover) to express a powerful spiritual message you believe is important for the world today.

Activity 4 Seeking peace with Christian spiritual music

An ancient song, recorded by many artists, is the Celtic Blessing:

> Deep peace of the running wave to you
>
> Deep peace of the quiet air to you
>
> Deep peace of the sacred earth to you
>
> Deep peace of the Son of Peace to you
>
> Deep peace.

- John Rutter and the 'Late Late Service' (to give examples from the classical and alternative worship traditions) are two examples of the way this song is loved today.

- Interestingly, it identifies four things that make for peace: three from the natural world and one that is religious.

- Begin by asking pupils to suggest four things that make the world more peaceful, and four that make the human heart more peaceful.

- Get them to be specific – not 'music' but 'this particular song' is the kind of answer that will be most helpful.

- Listen to the song with the class, in two versions if possible.

- Compare their responses to each version

- Ask the pupils to discuss how music is used to seek peace in Christian religion, and how they use music themselves.

- A good, open-ended way to report on this lesson is to ask pupils to write less than 200 words for homework in reply to these two questions: What did you do in RE today? What did you learn from it? The answers will show you some spiritual depth.

The creativity of a Muslim architect: the story of Hassan Fathy

For the teacher

RE teachers often express the concern that exemplars of Islamic faith are hard to find. Too frequently, the Muslim equivalents of Mother Teresa and Martin Luther King seem to be boxers: Muhammad Ali and Naseem Hamed. This work enables pupils to engage with a story of a Muslim who lived to serve the poorest in his community with his own professional skills.

This part of the book provides teaching and learning activities for 11–14s based upon the life story of Hassan Fathy, the controversial and greatly admired Islamic architect, who set aside fortune to develop a method of building for Egypt's peasant population. His 'architecture for the poor' was controversial in the 1940s and 50s, but with hindsight is seen as inspired and inspiring, ecologically sustainable and ahead of its time. Hassan Fathy was a 'liberation architect' before liberation theology existed, and a green architect before the word 'environmentalism' was coined in the West.

Creativity is sometimes too closely associated with visual art in school. But people are creative in their work, whether they are gardeners, architects or teachers. In a book about creativity and religion, it is appropriate to look at buildings for two reasons. First, because religions nearly always express their creative impulses in bricks and mortar: building sacred places is important. Second, because the buildings that communities create show the human concern for form and beauty in practical and everyday terms. Most people care more about their own home than about any work of art.

For pupils: a story and five activities

The main part of this work depends on pupils using the story of Hassan Fathy on the three following pages. Copy this for them, and consider how all pupils can best access the story. It may be useful to cut it up into the 10 paragraphs (pupils can sort and order them first if you like). Teachers telling stories do this better than merely reading them, but pupils may benefit from a written copy as well.

Assessing this work: 'I can…'

If pupils do this work thoughtfully, they may show achievement with regard to levels 3–5 of the English National Framework's eight-level scale.

Evidence of achievement: If pupils can say 'yes' to some of these, then they are working at the level indicated.

I can…

Level 3

- Describe how Hassan Fathy used his talents to help other people
- Make some links to the idea of a 'hero' for myself.

Level 4

- Describe the impact of some texts from the Qur'an on Hassan Fathy's work
- Describe what was inspiring to Hassan Fathy, and is inspiring to me.

Level 5

- Explain the impact of his religion on Hassan Fathy's work as an architect
- Express a range of views about 'sacred' building and helping other people.

See also: Hassan Fathy's work is well represented on the web. A search engine will give many starting points, but you might begin with these:

Hassan Fathy's life and work: www.geocities.com

Architectural photographs: www.archnet.org

The Aga Khan's Award site: www.akdn.org

The story of Hassan Fathy

Activity 1 Getting to grips with the story

(a) **Read it!** The story comes in ten paragraphs. In groups of five, each pupil reads aloud two each in turn. Get the feel of the story.

(b) **Summarise it!** Each pupil should summarise the two paragraphs they read in a single sentence each. Put these together and you have the whole story in a short 'ten sentence' form.

(c) **Discuss and agree:** What six words sum up Hassan's character? What did you like best about him?

(d) **Explain the impact of religion:** Find five ways in which he tried to put his Muslim beliefs into action.

Activity 2 Writing a citation

Work alone for this task. Hassan was nominated for the Aga Khan Award for Architecture in 1980, which he won. What do you think were Hassan's major achievements? Think about at least three things you think count as 'major achievements' and note them down, with reasons. Compare your list with a partner, and revise it if you want to. Argue out the best answers. Write a 100-word 'Citation' to be read out to the audience at Hassan's award ceremony. It should say briefly what won him the prize.

Activity 3 Defining a hero

Hassan didn't think he was a religious hero. He just saw himself as a Muslim trying to do his job well, for the benefit of ordinary people. Do you think Hassan is a hero? What makes a hero to you?

Activity 4 Respect the text

Here are three quotations from the Holy Qur'an. Do you think Hassan Fathy is an example of how to put these into action? Give explanations of your ideas.

Activity 5 School and soul

Consider Hassan's idea that a school building should be a place for the soul to grow. Is your school building like this? Draw up a list of 10 ways the building could be more like a 'soul growth' place.

Simplified quotations from the Holy Quran	I think this applies to Hassan Fathy's story because….
'Those who spend their wealth on God's ways are like a grain that grows seven ears, and each ear a hundred more grains. God gives increase! Those who spend their wealth in pursuit of the pleasure of Allah are like a garden that brings forth fruit.' (2:261, 264)	
'A good deed is like a good tree whose root is firmly planted in the earth, whose branches reach to the heavens; it brings forth fruit in season through the care of the person who tends it.' (14:24-5)	
'The righteous are those who believe in Allah, and give their wealth for the love of Him to the orphans, the needy and the traveller.' (2:177)	

© 2008 RE Today Services
Permission is granted to photocopy this page for use in classroom activities in schools that have purchased this publication.

REtoday
Services

Hassan Fathy's story: mud bricks versus concrete

What would you do with a million pounds?

Hassan was born in 1900. His wealthy parents lived in the Egyptian city of Cairo, and each summer they travelled south with their growing son to Alexandria for holidays. From the windows of the train, Hassan watched the countryside and its poor people passing by, and dreamed of what he would do if he was a millionaire. He had two dreams: one was to hire a yacht big enough to carry an orchestra and sail the world while he listened to his favourite music. The other dream was to build a perfect village for the peasants of the land to live in. He imagined the tame lambs being fed by the children in the market squares. In Cairo, the only lambs he saw were going to be butchered for meat.

Making a difference When he grew older, Hassan went to university. His first choice of career was to study agriculture, but he had lived in the city, not the country, and he fluffed his interview because he had never been near a field. Architecture was his second choice. His first job in the 1920s was to design a new school in Talkha, a small town in the delta of the river Nile. For the first time, he saw what could go wrong in the countryside: no one was feeding lambs by hand in the marketplace. Instead, narrow muddy streets infested with flies were the only playground for sick-looking ragged children. Hassan couldn't bear to walk through the streets and made his way to work each day by skirting the whole town. He realised that Egypt's peasants were typical of hundreds of millions all over the world: 'abandoned by God and man, they dragged out their short, diseased and ugly lives in dirt and discomfort', he wrote. Although an architect could become rich through working in the city on modern buildings, Hassan felt drawn to help the peasants who lived on the land. He determined to make a difference.

Farms, roofing and mud In the next ten years, Hassan first reformed the farms owned by his own rich family, so that the peasants who lived and worked there could live in clean and more pleasant homes. He discovered that the old rural traditions of building with bricks made of mud and straw were dying out as concrete and cement became more common building materials (though they were expensive). Egyptians had built with mud brick since the days of the pyramids 5000 years earlier. Hassan became convinced that a better life for thousands of villagers would come from villagers building their own homes properly with mud brick rather than from using expensive concrete panels. He built some wonderful mansions for rich clients out of traditional materials. He made mud brick trendy! When the war started in 1939, suddenly steel, timber and concrete were impossible to get. Mud bricks were all that was left. One problem was making roofs with mud brick. Hassan's first attempt was supported by wooden scaffolding during the building. When they took the scaffolding down, the roof collapsed as well.

© 2008 RE Today Services
Permission is granted to photocopy this page for use in classroom activities in schools that have purchased this publication.

Ancient building crafts rediscovered Hassan knew that in the villages there were still some older builders who could make lovely domed roofs out of mud. He went to Aswan to find out how it was done, and was thrilled to find people who still knew the older ways. At Luxor, he found beautiful mud-brick domes and two-storey buildings that had been there for over 3000 years. This disproved the city architects' view that mud-brick buildings could not last. He learned from the peasants that to build a sound, long-lasting house from mud cost only a quarter of the price of a concrete and steel city home. As his interest in the beautiful buildings of ancient Egypt grew, Hassan found opportunities to prove his theories that 'simple' can be cheap and beautiful. After a flood destroyed 25 peasant houses in a village near Cairo, the Red Crescent charity asked Hassan to build a new one. His mud-brick building was airy, light, beautiful and built to last.

A whole new village The government engaged Hassan for a much bigger project. Gourna was a large village in the famous Valley of the Kings, site of all the ancient Pharaohs' tombs, populated by about 7000 people. They made their livings by robbing the tombs. To save the ancient sites and to change the lives of the people of Gourna it was decided to build them a whole new village. Hassan was given the job, because his mud-brick plans could be both beautiful and cheap. He planned to use the 50-acre site of New Gourna to create an environment and village where the good life could flourish. The beautiful mud-brick buildings used ancient but rediscovered ways of keeping cool and fresh in a desert climate. Cunning wind-catchers brought breezes into the houses. Latticed windows let the air flow, but kept the sand out. Hassan wanted to train the villagers to create their own homes as well. He felt sure that people could look after themselves, without needing charity, if they were given the chance to train. He began classes so that hundreds of people who had formerly been thieves could become builders, roofers or brickmakers. One of the newly trained masons began to save money for the first time in his life. When he had enough, he fulfilled his lifetime dream: he went to Makkah on the pilgrimage.

Health through architecture The dreadful disease of bilharzia was one problem Hassan was sure he could solve. He designed the village water supplies to prevent contamination and disease from spreading. He noticed the sayings of the Prophet: 'Bring up your children to learn to ride horses and to swim'. Hassan couldn't provide horses for every village, but he did make sure that Gourna had a clean swimming pool for the children. This was unknown in the poor rural communities of Egypt. To make sure that people understood the danger of disease, Hassan made up a play for the children.

He dressed up as 'Bill Harzia', an evil demon in a gas mask who haunts a baby boy up to the age of 10 before striking him down with disease. Two doctors race to the rescue, and slay the demon. The children are warned that the evil Bill lurks in unsafe and dirty water everywhere. Not many highly qualified architects dress up for children's plays!

Green architecture Hassan knew that many rich Egyptians wanted air-conditioning and heating systems in their homes, to be like the wealthy Western world – the USA for example. But he was more interested in traditional ways of keeping cool and keeping warm. He talked to peasant builders about this, and rediscovered the art of the 'malkaf' or 'wind-catcher'. In the school at Gourna he tried the idea out. Setting a kind of chimney in the building, angled at the prevailing wind, he could bring cool, fresh air from high above ground into the school for ventilation. He set up a charcoal panel, with a tap to wet it, at the top of the 'malkaf' so that the air flowed over the panel, making it even cooler. He said 'for the Arab, the kindly aspect of nature is the sky, pure, clean, promising coolness and life giving water, dwarfing the desert with the starry infinite. It's no wonder that for desert dwellers, the sky became the home of God.'

Building a mosque: The village of new Gourna needed a mosque. Hassan wanted it to serve the worshippers, shielding them from the outside world, and showing the direction of Makkah. A plain design would help people to concentrate upon Allah in their prayers, and the Islamic tradition of using beautiful design patterns and calligraphy meant that walls could be decorated with the word of Allah: 'the worshipper is led back all the time to the word of god' he said. He believed that religious architecture reflects the ideas that the community has about what is holy, so he built in the ancient style of upper Egypt. Hassan also wanted the mosque to be a community focus, so he built a long passage at the side of the mosque, shaded with a barrel vault, and provided with water jars, where people could meet and share friendship.

Building a school: 'If love goes into the work, it will always show. The school is like a mosque or a church: it is a place for children's souls to grow, and the building must invite them in, not cramp them. The architect has a grave duty of creating in a building a source of love and encouragement for children.' With these thoughts, Hassan made a beautiful courtyard for the school, with classrooms designed around it. High windows provided restful light, and mud-brick domes made higher, more beautiful ceilings. Hassan hoped the children would find the ornamental ponds, the garden areas and the small, child-friendly scale of the building would help them to learn well. Three of the 'beautiful ninety-nine names of Allah' that Muslims use are 'the Maker, the Provider, the Kindly One.'

The architect who cared for the poor: In later life, Hassan came to look back on his buildings at Gourna as an unfulfilled vision. The village never worked as he had hoped it would. But he wrote 'I prostrated myself in prayer to the Almighty, thanking him for his gift. The Qur'an says: "if you give thanks, you will be given yet more".' Hassan was given more. He became a very famous architect, received a doctorate, travelled the world, and designed many beautiful buildings. He was awarded the internationally famous 'Aga Khan Award for Architecture' in 1980. He stayed true to his ideals: co-operate with the poorest people, respect the skills of working people, build a better society, listen to others, use the land and materials that are nearby.

© 2008 RE Today Services
Permission is granted to photocopy this page for use in classroom activities in schools that have purchased this publication.

Places of national religious significance: exploring what makes a spiritual place famous

For the teacher

- What is a 'place of national religious significance'?
- What beliefs are expressed in these places?
- How could I express religious significance creatively?

The activity outlined in this section will enable your pupils to think for themselves about what makes some places spiritual. It is fun and, while the entry points are simple, it provides opportunities to use and develop a range of skills: speaking and listening, critical thinking, and forming sound judgements.

The English *National Framework for RE* (non statutory) says that pupils aged 11–14 should, where possible, visit a place of national religious significance. What would such places be? This activity offers a creative thinking approach to such places. It leads towards a compelling learning activity in which pupils design a place of major religious or spiritual significance.

See also ...

1. Sacred destinations

This website is an excellent access point to a large number of places of worship.

www.sacred-destinations.com

2. Places of worship

This website provides a range of resources to support visiting places of worship, e.g. videos, guidelines for planning a visit, assessment, and a search facility to identify 'places near you'.

http://pow.reonline.org.uk

3. Learning Outside the Classroom Manifesto

The LOTC Manifesto sets out the educational benefits of enabling every young person to experience the world outside their classroom as an essential part of their learning and personal development.

www.teachernet.gov.uk/learningoutsidetheclassroom

Evidence of achievements

Pupils can demonstrate achievement at levels 4–7 in these activities, if they can say 'yes' to some of these 'I can...' statements.

Level 4: I can...

- use words and ideas about places that are religiously significant to show my understanding of why these places matter to large numbers of people in Britain today
- apply the idea of a place of religious or spiritual significance to a design of my own, thoughtfully.

Level 5: I can...

- explain why some people would choose non religious places as spiritually significant
- explain similarities and differences between my 'top three' places of religious or spiritual significance
- express my own views about the idea of 'sacred spaces' using religious and spiritual terminology thoughtfully.

Level 6: I can...

- give an informed account of what makes a place 'of national religious significance'
- interpret the meanings and significance of three places of **religious** significance for myself, explaining why they matter to their communities clearly
- express my own insights into the diverse places that are significant in religion in Britain today; express insights into the difference between 'spiritual' and 'religious' places
- respond to the challenges of describing sacred places in a plural society.

Level 7: I can...

- use the methods of sociology of religion to give coherent accounts of different understandings of sacred places
- use a wide religious vocabulary to explain my personal and critical evaluation of what makes places 'of national religious (or spiritual) significance'.

Three activities about places of national significance in RE

Introduction

- The activity presents 12 candidates for the title 'place of major religious or spiritual significance'. All these places have websites that illustrate their attractions and importance.

- Ask 12 groups of two or three pupils each to begin by exploring the relevant website and identifying reasons why their place has significance for the whole country.

- There is a PowerPoint presentation on the RE Today subscribers' website to support this activity, which includes visual materials about all 12 of the places in the activity.

Activity 1 A class debate on the possible places of national religious significance

- Arrange for pupils in groups of two or three to investigate one of the places suggested on pages 17 and 18, preparing a speaker in the group to make a case for their place. Spend one lesson on this research exploration, and ask pupils to complete their presentation for homework. Criteria such as these can be used: Is the place spiritually atmospheric? Does it have a role in history? Does it have a role in the present and future of British religion? Does this place stir deep and spiritual feelings for many people? Is this place unique?

- One of the group can then speak for 90 seconds to the whole class, explaining why their chosen place should receive high scores and top votes. Take classroom votes on which places should be in the top six, and which is the most significant of them all.

Activity 2 Individual pupils select and account for their own choices

- In class debates, individuals may feel nudged in certain directions by the group. For this second activity, ask pupils to choose three of the places on the list of 12 (or they might choose two from the list and add a third of their own choosing) and plan a pilgrimage to visit them.

  o What order would they go in and why?

  o What would be their spiritual hopes and focus as they travelled?

  o Who would be good companions for the journey?

  o What music and reading would complement the trip?

Activity 3 Groups plan and design places of national religious or spiritual significance for the twenty-first century

- Working again in a group of four, pupils are given the design brief on page 19. Encourage them to draw upon the ideas they have been exploring in Activities 1 and 2 and to develop detailed applications and ideas about spiritual or sacred space for themselves.

- The brief details of eight aspects of this work are given on page 19, but students should be encouraged to develop their ideas through this compelling learning activity, and use skills from other curriculum areas such as design technology or music to bring their best ideas to life. The focus on the emotions of worship and the human need for calmness and reflection seek to get to the heart of what sacred space is for.

RE Today weblink:

www.retoday.org.uk

The RE Today subscribers' website has a free download, a PowerPoint presentation in which some of these activities are introduced to pupils through a trial in school. If you're a subscriber, check *REtoday* for your password and help yourself to this.

Places of national religious significance – why might they be?

Stonehenge is a place of major spiritual significance because of its antiquity. It's distinctively British, a stone circle dating back 5000 years, and it has a wonderful way of connecting people to the ancient spiritual traditions of the country.

It's an inclusive space: anyone can be spiritual at Stonehenge, you don't have to be religious. Stonehenge is British. It simply wouldn't mean much to people from other nations. It is mysterious, and makes any visitor ask questions and wonder at the beauty of the sunrise through its arches.

www.stonehenge.co.uk

Shree Sanatan Mandir, Leicester is a place of major religious significance in the UK today because it's one of the oldest and biggest Hindu mandirs in the country. It doesn't represent only one part of the community: there are shrines to many different gods and goddesses.

It has a long history, and the building used to be a Christian chapel as well. It houses the headquarters of the National Council of Hindu Temples. School parties from all over the Midlands visit almost every day to see *puja* worship for themselves.

www.
sanatanmandirleicester.com

Samye Ling Buddhist Centre in Dumfries in Scotland is a place of major spiritual significance because it's a place where Buddhists and those interested in Buddhism meet and share ideas. Thousands of Buddhists, and thousands of other people, go there for peace, reflection and compassion every year.

The work of the centre in its stunning Scottish hillside setting includes health and healing as well as meditation and education. School trips mean that lots of young people learn from Buddhism for themselves at Samye Ling.

www.samyeling.org

Manchester Jewish Museum is a place of major spiritual significance because it records and celebrates the long history of Jewish people in the UK. The Grade 2 listed building was a synagogue for over a century from 1874 until it reopened as a museum over twenty years ago.

Thousands of visitors to the museum learn the rich heritage of Judaism in Britain and explore their own attitudes to Jewish life and faith.

www.
manchesterjewishmuseum.
com

Coventry Cathedral is a place of major spiritual significance because after the bombing of the old cathedral by the Nazis in the war, the new cathedral rose from the ashes and was created as a sign of forgiveness and reconciliation.

It isn't just a place of Christian worship: it's for the city and the nation, and it shows how old enemies can be reconciled. Brilliant art, glass, sculpture and architecture make it special.

www.coventrycathedral.org.
uk

St Mungo's Museum of Religious Life and Art is a place of major spiritual significance because it is Glasgow's inter-faith space, where religions meet. Art rather than worship is its function, so it helps religions to share their ideas, not refuse to meet, to be at peace rather than to fight.

The museum houses a prize exhibit: Salvador Dali's brilliant painting called 'Christ of St John of the Cross'

At www.glasgow.gov.
uk choose Museums – St Mungo's

© 2008 RE Today Services
Permission is granted to photocopy this page for use in classroom activities in schools that have purchased this publication.

The **Beth Shalom Holocaust Museum in Nottinghamshire** is a place of major spiritual significance because it is a centre for remembrance of the worst genocide in human history. It was founded by Christians, but works closely with the Jewish and Christian communities.

No one should forget the holocaust. Beth Shalom means that people will remember it, and learn from it for many years to come.
www.bethshalom.com
www.holocaustcentre.net

Hope Street, Liverpool (the Roman Catholic Cathedral is at one end and the Anglican Cathedral at the other) is a place of major spiritual significance because it is a symbol of the new unity of Christians. It joins a brilliant twentieth-century Catholic cathedral with a wonderful nineteenth-century Anglican one, and is a sign of hope for anyone who wants religious unity.
The Anglican Cathedral:
www.liverpoolcathedral.org.uk
The Roman Catholic Cathedral:
www.liverpoolmetrocathedral.org.uk

Regents Park Mosque is a key Muslim centre, open for over 30 years. The land was given to the Muslim communities in 1944, recognising how Muslims had fought with the British Empire in the war. The Islamic Cultural Centre began then, and the London Central Mosque was opened in 1977.

Hundreds of thousands visit and pray here each year. Islam is the second largest religion in the country with 1.6 million followers so it's a place of major religious significance to British Muslims.

The best starting point for this is the Islamic Cultural Centre:
www.iccuk.org

St Paul's Cathedral is a place of major spiritual significance because of its history and splendour. Previous cathedrals and churches made the site sacred many hundreds of years ago. Sir Christopher Wren's 300-year-old dome survived the Nazi blitz in the war, and it was used for the Prince Charles' wedding in 1982.

It's the place for faith to be celebrated in the nation. It's iconic and beautiful, even more than many other UK cathedrals. It's also a dynamic cultural centre in the heart of the city of London. www.stpauls.co.uk
www.stpauls.co.uk

The **Gurdwara Shri Guru Singh Sabha in Hounslow** is a place of major spiritual significance because it is the produce of the endeavour of the Sikh community and it brings a little of India to London.

Half a million Sikhs look to Hounslow for inspiration. The Gurdwara is a centre not just for Sikh religion, but for social action, education, community care and celebration and festivities. It celebrates Sikh life for the whole nation.
www.sgss.org

Snowden, North Wales is not a religious place, but many thousands of people test their strength on Snowdon, Wales' tallest mountain, each year. When they get to the top, they often experience a feeling of spiritual fulfilment.

Millions of people get their spiritual sense from the world of nature rather than from churches or mosques. Snowden should be in this list to represent that spirituality of connecting with the beauties and wonders of the natural environment.
www.snowdoniaguide.com

© 2008 RE Today Services
Permission is granted to photocopy this page for use in classroom activities in schools that have purchased this publication.

Stonehenge

Shree Sanatan Mandir, Leicester

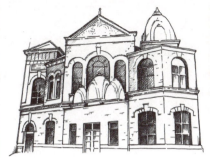

Samye Ling Buddhist Centre in Dumfries

Manchester Jewish Museum

Coventry Cathedral

St Mungo's Museum of Religious Life and Art

The Beth Shalom Holocaust Museum in Nottinghamshire

Hope Street, Liverpool

Regents Park Mosque

St Paul's Cathedral

The Gurdwara Shri Guru Singh Sabha in Hounslow

Snowden, North Wales

© 2008 RE Today Services
Permission is granted to photocopy this page for use in classroom activities in schools that have purchased this publication.

Creating a sacred space for the twenty-first century: spiritual architecture

The brief

- **Introduction:** Religious buildings have very specific architecture, which usually arises out of the beliefs and needs of the community that will use them. Increasingly, public institutions like prisons, airports, colleges and hospitals create shared sacred spaces that can be used by more than one religious community, or by non-religious people, for reflection or community celebration. Following your study of what gives a place national religious significance, you can decide what kind of building it will be – a shared space, or one for a particular faith community.

- **Task:** Working in small group you are invited to take on the role of architects, and to **plan and design a new spiritual place**. The eight boxes below will guide you through the task.

Designing sacred space on the computer

- Use a graphics package to make careful images of the spiritual design your group has produced.

- Think about the planning, details, uses of the building and the ways that space becomes sacred to a community through their use of the building.

Artistic expression in sacred space

- Will your sacred place use the arts for expressing spirituality?

- Sculpture, tapestry, or specially commissioned artwork is common in many religious traditions. Can one of your team work on paintings, stonework, stained glass art or some other form?

Space enclosed or open to the skies?

- How will your spiritual place use the natural environment?

- Being open to the skies, and using plants and trees, water and flowers, is very important in some people's spiritual life. Natural light can matter a lot as well. How can your designs be 'green', and make the most of the natural?

News about your design for the web

- Many places of religious significance have a website or newsletter which publicises all their activities.

- Using your notes and research, and your imagination, design the website or newsletter for your new building, illustrating all that might go on there.

Welcoming? Celebrating? Music? Food?

- Draw careful plans of the inside of the new sacred space.

- Show the arrangements you have made for welcoming young and old, for celebrations and community events, weddings or funerals, music and food.

Worship with many and with few

- What kind of seating arrangements will you make? Will people be comfortable when the place is crowded?

- How will everyone be able to feel part of what goes on at a big celebration, but not lost in a small act of worship?

Shared holy space?

- One of the hardest challenges for your team of architects is dealing with religious diversity. Will your sacred space be for any religion? Can Muslims and Buddhists use it? Would an agnostic or an atheist find it a calm and reflective space? Decide how you want to respond to this challenge.

- Check out your ideas with people from different belief groups if you can.

Symbolism for everyone

- Think about the symbolism that you use. Symbols of rock, fire, water, growth, life and death are common in many spiritual places. What will you suggest, design and use in your spiritual space?

- Find some examples to inspire you, and design your own. Stained glass ideas, for example, look beautiful made of coloured tissue paper, displayed on a window.

© 2008 RE Today Services
Permission is granted to photocopy this page for use in classroom activities in schools that have purchased this publication.

Poetry, creativity and learning about Easter

For the teacher

In this article, Claire Clinton, RE adviser from Newham, provides some strategies for using the work of the Christian poet Steve Turner to explore the meaning and theology of Easter. These activities are based on some of Steve's poems, and build upon students' knowledge of the Passion narrative in the gospels. The following extracts and notes will help your students.

- Matthew's Gospel chapter 27: verses 27-31 (The soldiers mock Jesus)
- 27:32-44 (The crucifixion)
- 27:45-56 (The death of Jesus)
- 27:57-61 (The burial of Jesus)
- 27:62-66 (The guard at the tomb)
- 28:1-10 (The resurrection).

Points of explanation from the New International Version text:

- v.28: scarlet/red was a royal colour in the first century CE, so the soldiers were being sarcastic by putting this on Jesus.

- v.35: casting lots was like a dice game played in the first century.

- v.46: some Christians believe that Jesus was separated from his heavenly Father at this point. He had taken on himself the sins of the world. He was the sacrifice that Christians believe means that their sins can be forgiven.

- v.51: the curtain referred to here was in the Jewish temple in Jerusalem, dividing the inner court from the 'Holy of Holies' (the place where Jewish people believed the presence of God dwelt). This tearing of the curtain symbolises the Christian belief that through Jesus all people can gain access to the presence of God.

  Pupils will learn a lot from watching some film extracts. Seeing how one part of the story is created in two different films is a useful way to get students to think about the meaning behind the story; for example you could use:

- *The Miracle Maker* (from the Bible Society)
- Zefferelli's *Jesus of Nazareth*
- *The Last Temptation of Christ*
- *The Passion of the Christ* (take care with these last two – they have an 18 certificate).

Achievements is shown in this work with reference to these 'I can...' statements

Level 4: I can...

- show that I understand some meanings of the Easter celebrations for different Christians

- use key vocabulary, concepts and ways of expressing meaning to apply Christian beliefs to Easter activities.

Level 5: I can...

- suggest reasons for similar and different beliefs within Christianity concerning Easter

- use a wide range of key words or images to explain similarities and differences in how Christians express beliefs about Easter

- compare my beliefs with those of others about Easter.

Level 6: I can...

- suggest interpretations of Easter stories and events, explaining reasons for diversity

- explain some ways in which Christian beliefs about Easter have an impact on British society today

- compare my beliefs with those of others about Easter and life after death, evaluating one challenge for a Christian when celebrating Easter.

Interview with a poet, Steve Turner

Q: Thinking about 'Poem for Easter', and 'Christmas is Really for the Children', do you still like these two poems?

A: I can't image rewriting them. There is nothing that I look at in these poems and want to rewrite them.

Q: What makes a poem good?

A: For a poem to be good it has to succeed in what you intended it to do. Sometimes it might simply be an emotion of a view that you want to express. At other times you set yourself a technical challenge. The best poems are probably a combination of the two. Determining what is or isn't a 'proper poem' is something people will always argue about. I read my poems out loud to myself and get a sense of when it's finished that must be similar to the sense a musician gets as to when a piece of music is complete. It just feels right. You feel there is nothing more to add.

With the 'Poem for Easter' my technical challenge was to say something true about the death and resurrection of Christ using the familiar patter of an old-style comedian. As you can imagine, it's quite hard to use humour with such a momentous subject without making light of what you're talking about. 'Christmas is Really for the Children' began with the title. Sometimes I'll take a cliché like that and play with it. Of course after playing with it I actually subvert it because the point of the poem is that Christmas is *not* just for children!

Q: How do these two poems show your Christian beliefs?

A: In the Bible there is a strong theme about remembering, remembering great events, for example events that happened to the Israelites and the fact that they built something at these locations to remember the story or event. Remembering is a good thing. When the disciples wanted to build a memorial to the transfiguration, Jesus said 'no', and so I don't believe Christians have to be bound by going to certain places to remember a story or a certain time. The good news is that Jesus can be with me all day, every day.

Q: So does Christmas Day or Easter matter to you?

A: Personally I think about Christ's coming into the world and his death every day. I don't really mark it as a special day – I don't think of it more on 25 December more than 25 March. I know that some people find the church calendar helpful. I go to a Church of England church so there are special services always to ensure that we do think about every part of Jesus' life and death during each year. The important thing in the Christian story is that Jesus is a historical figure – he died a death but, unlike any other historical figure, Christians claim that he overcame death and is still alive. He still exists in the universe today. If he had died and that was it, Christians would have to evaluate him as an inspirational leader, a great thinker, or a philosopher. He couldn't do any more for you than Aristotle or Plato can do for you now. He would leave behind his ideas, which may be thought of as 'great', but that would be all. The difference between philosophy and Jesus is that philosophy says 'This is the way': Jesus says 'I am the way'.

Can death ever be liberating?

Create a pyramid shape using the quotation cards your teacher will give you. Place the quotation you like best at the top, then two quotations you like best next below it, and finally the three you agree with least on the bottom level.

> 'Dying is a very dull, dreary affair. And my advice to you is to have nothing whatever to do with it.'
>
> W Somerset Maugham

> 'The day which we fear as our last is but the birthday of eternity.'
>
> Seneca

> 'Some people are so afraid to die that they never begin to live.'
>
> Henry Van Dyke

> 'Death may be the greatest of all human blessings.'
>
> Socrates

> 'No one can confidently say that he will still be living tomorrow.'
>
> Euripides

> 'All religions are the same: religion is basically guilt, with different holidays.'
>
> Cathy Ladman

Steve Turner wrote the poem 'Death Lib' when he had the thought 'Could there be anything great about death?' The rest of the poem flowed from that one thought. Now read this poem.

Death Lib

The liberating thing about death

Is in its fairness to women

Its acceptance of blacks

Its special consideration for the sick.

And I like the way

That children aren't excluded

Homosexuals are welcomed

And militants aren't banned.

The really wonderful thing about death

Is that all the major religions agree on it

All beliefs take you there

All philosophy bows before it

All arguments end there.

Con men can't con it

Thieves can't nick it

Bullies can't share it

Magicians can't trick it.

Boxers can't punch it

Nor critics dismiss it

Don't knows can't not know

The lazy can't miss it.

Governments can't ban it

Or the army defuse it

Judges can't jail it

Lawyers can't sue it.

Capitalists can't bribe it

Socialists can't share it

Terrorists can't jump it

The third world aren't spared it.

Scientists can't quell it

Nor can they disprove it

Doctors can't cure it

Surgeons can't move it.

Einstein can't halve it

Guevara can't free it

The thing about dead

Is we're all gonna be it.

Activity

1. With a partner, discuss what you believe happens after a person dies. What symbol for death would you choose?

2. What do you think of Steve's poem? Give your view of the strengths, weaknesses and questions it raises.

3. Using a copy of the table on the next page as well as the information file for some clues, tick the columns that apply to different religious and secular views on death.

© 2008 RE Today Services
Permission is granted to photocopy this page for use in classroom activities in schools that have purchased this publication.

REtoday
Services

What people believe about life after death: who believe in…	Atheist	Buddhist	Christian	Hindu	Jewish	Muslim	Sikh
Heaven							
Hell							
Annihilation	✓						
Transmigration of the soul							
Reincarnation		✓					

Information file

All religions hold one or more of the following beliefs about a person's life after they die:

- **Heaven:** Eternity is spent in heaven or paradise with God, in a state that is beautiful beyond our ability to conceive.

- **Hell:** Eternity is spent in hell with Satan and his demons. All are tormented and tortured, in isolation from God, without any hope of mercy or relief.

- **Annihilation:** The body rots. One's soul, spirit, memory, personality, awareness, body and mind disappear and are no more. Some religious people believe that this takes place after God's judgement if you are not to enter heaven.

- **Transmigration of the soul:** One's soul and spirit are reborn into a human foetus or newborn child.

- **Reincarnation:** One's soul and spirit are reborn into another living entity – not necessarily human.

Religious and secular worldviews have many different beliefs about what happens when someone dies. One of the things **Christians** believe about death is that it is not necessarily the end of human life. **Christians believe in life after death**, and that they can access this through Jesus' death on the cross and his resurrection. Every religious and secular worldview has a founder, but Christians are unique in wanting to say that their founder is still alive and he came back from the dead. This is the belief that is celebrated in churches around the world on a daily and weekly basis, but Easter, the most important festival, is where Christians may focus on thinking a little bit more about what Jesus' death and resurrection means for them.

> **The thing about dead
> Is we're all gonna be it.**
>
> Steve Turner's last two
> lines from 'Death Lib'

Task

Imagine an Atheist and a Buddhist meet with a Christian and a Hindu and get talking about life after death. Can you write one question they would all agree on the answer to, and one question they would all have a different answer to? Script their conversation, to present to the class.

 © 2008 RE Today Services
Permission is granted to photocopy this page for use in classroom activities in schools that have purchased this publication.

What is Easter for?

Imagine you are a Christian who has been asked to choose a poem about Easter to be read out to your year group. You have been given a choice between these two poems: which one would you choose and why? Within a small group, discuss your reasons for your choice.

Poem for Easter

Tell me

What came first

Easter or the egg?

Crucifixion or daffodils?

Three days in a tomb

Or four days in Paris?

(returning bank holiday Monday).

When is a door not a door?

When it is rolled away

When is a body not a body?

When it is a risen.

Question.

Why was it the saviour

rode on the cross?

Answer.

to get us

to the other side

Behold I stand

Behold I stand and what?

Behold I stand at the door and

Knock Knock.

Christmas is Really for the Children

Christmas is really for the children.

Especially the children

who like animals, stables,

stars and babies

wrapped in swaddling clothes.

Then there are wise men

kings in fine robes

humble shepherds and a

hint of rich perfume.

Easter is not really for the children

unless accompanied by

a cream filled egg.

It has whips, blood, nails,

a spear and allegations

of body snatching.

It involves politics, God and

the sins of the world.

It is not good for people

of a nervous disposition.

They would do better to

think on rabbits, chickens

and the first snowdrop

of spring.

Or they'd do better to

wait for a re-run of

Christmas without asking

too many questions about

what Jesus did when he grew up

or whether there's any

connection.

For small group discussion

Find out which poem was most chosen and the reasons people gave for choosing it.

1. Was the poem chosen because it was easier to understand?

2. What makes a poem a really good poem?

3. How does each of the poems help to explain what Christians believe about Easter?

Either:

4. Can you create a collage or a 14-line poem to express why Easter is important to Christians? It could be used in your school with your year group or with younger pupils.

Or:

5. 'Easter is not good for people of a nervous disposition.' Discuss this quotation from one of Steve's poems, making sure that you refer to views that would agree and disagree with his comment on Easter.

RE Today weblink:

www.retoday.org.uk

There are extra resources on-line for activities on Easter available to RE Today subscribers at www.retoday.org.uk. Passwords are printed in *REtoday* each term.

© 2008 RE Today Services
Permission is granted to photocopy this page for use in classroom activities in schools that have purchased this publication.

Explore a poem in RE

Warm up activity: 'Who am I?' Stick a name onto the back of every student in the class. They must try and find out who they are by asking questions of other students to which the other student can only answer 'yes' or 'no'.

Stimulus: Read out the poem to the class. You could have it displayed on the interactive white board too, along with the key word definitions

7/8 of the Truth and Nothing but the Truth

If you are sitting comfortably

I suspect I am not giving you

The truth.

I am leaving you two poems

Short of disagreement

So that you can remark upon

The likeness of our minds.

I am being kind

I am giving you truth

In linctus form – strawberry flavour

I am being unkind

I am ignoring the correct dosage.

I want to be liked

That's my trouble.

I want to be agreed with.

I know you all like strawberry

I quite like it myself.

It's nothing but the truth

But it's not the whole truth.

No one admires the whole truth.

No one ever applauds

It takes things too far.

It's nice, but where would

You put it?

People who neglect the strawberry

flavouring do not get asked back

They get put in their place

With nails if necessary.

Steve Turner

Key word: *Linctus is another word for medication. So a brand of strawberry linctus you would have heard of is 'Calpol'. We flavour children's medicine so that they will want to swallow it; we make it sweet, because the real medicine tastes disgusting without the sugar!*

Questions to think about in pairs:

Choose at least three of these questions to talk about:

- What is this poem about?
- Who is the poem about?
- Is truth always uncomfortable to hear? To read? To see? Give some examples.
- Does everyone like agreeing with people more than disagreeing?
- Why does disagreement upset us?
- What analogy does the poet use to talk about truth? Is it a good one?
- Is the truth we like similar to a child's form of strawberry flavour medicine?
- 'No one admires the whole truth'. Is that true? Does it take things too far?
- Does the truth need to be sweetened?
- Is it always good to tell with whole truth and nothing but the truth? Reasons?

RE Today weblink:

www.retoday.org.uk

Additional resources on the RE Today website present this poem as a stimulus for a 'Philosophy for Children' enquiry.

Teaching Islamic art: ideas for the secondary classroom

For the teacher

The spiritual dimensions are too often neglected in our schools. Both faith and non-faith schools pay very little attention to this important field. Spiritual education is more than a strict discipline: it should underpin all of school life. You can't assess or implement spiritual education in any given institution through policy and monitoring alone. I believe that timeless traditional ways of being spiritual need to be built into the fabric of learning rather than merely using a template. This article shows teachers how to use Islamic calligraphy as a spiritual discipline. Can pupils show their spiritual qualities, such as attentiveness and care, in making letters on paper?

Before doing anything else, I want you to step back and reflect for a moment on 'Teaching Christian Art'. How would you define it? And what exactly would you begin to teach? It's quite tricky isn't it? So often we forget how rich religious art is. For instance, would you get children to look at medieval Christian art or perhaps study a modern Christian artist? Could pupils make art that was Christian, or just learn from it? Then again, what would your lesson objective be? Would you talk about faith or the artistic style of the individual?

It's these sorts of questions that are on my mind when I'm asked to introduce Islamic art in the classroom. Over the years, in teaching Islamic art to pupils, I've found that calligraphy is a great way to introduce the visual crafts of Islam. I usually start by teaching basic letters and then get children to experiment with making their own designs. It's much more creative than just allowing children to copy arabesques and patterns.

In the classroom

This article presents some simple, tried and tested starting points. Copiable pages from page 27 to 30 will enable pupils aged 11–12 to practise and make progress with some simple calligraphy. Link the work to their learning about Islamic understandings of Allah. Arabic is the language of the Qur'an. Muslims believe that the Angel Jibra'il (Gabriel) brought down the actual words from God to humankind through Prophet Muhammad, peace be upon him.

Islamic art

One of the outstanding characteristics of Islamic art most talked about, is the prescription against drawing animate images of human beings and other living creatures. However it's really important to know that Islamic art did not arise from restrictions on making these sorts of images. There are many other reasons why Muslims don't engage in realist art, but use Arabic and patterns. There has been a great debate in Islam, as to whether images of human beings and animate living beings are acceptable. This view can be found in other religions as well.

There are many views within Islam. Some Muslims do not believe any image of a human or animate creature is acceptable. While Muslims who believe that photographs are simply images like reflections wouldn't find a problem with photographs or TV pictures, others believe that eyes should not be represented but the body can be. Yet others deliberately create imperfections in their designs.

Further information and lesson aids can be found in *Islamic Art: The Teacher's Book* by Razwan Ul-Haq, and you can download Islamic artwork for free from his website www.ulhaqbrothers.com

Activity 1 The interview

> Razwan Ul-Haq reflects on his artistic work in the light of his Muslim faith. Read the interview and then work with a partner on your own interview.

Q: Does creativity fit well with faith?

A: Some people feel that creativity and faith are at loggerheads; however, religious experience tends to happen in the 'image' section of the individual, and for this reason I've always found religious people very interesting and hugely creative. They tend to trust their souls more and thus tap into the 'reservoir of spiritual expanse'.

Q: You're a creative person yourself. In what ways has Islamic faith influenced your creativity and art?

A: I would say that Islamic faith has had a huge impact on my creativity. The fact that I use Arabic calligraphy primarily is directly as a result of the fact that the Muslim holy book, the Qur'an, is in Arabic. Secondly, the cosmological view of the world and the spirit as offered through the Muslim worldview has influenced what I have to say. For instance, the world is temporal, and not permanent, therefore my art attempts to show the superiority of the spirit over matter. It tends to be impressionist and abstract, it doesn't attempt to glorify the beauty of the world but seeks the Other beauty. For me, as a Muslim, the soul is more important than the body, and the next world (hereafter) is more significant than today's world. In terms of poetry, I am concerned with illustrating the spiritual side of life. In my four novels (The Last Sufi series) all the poetry is composed to direct one's heart towards the Creator.

Q: When people copy the beautiful names, would you say that can be worship? What kind of mental state is needed for this?

A: For a Muslim, worship should happen throughout the day. The Prophet Muhammad ﷺ has said that even the act of smiling pleasantly to someone or removing a stone from a road so that it will not hurt people is an act of worship. If you look on my website (Classics Gallery) you can see my calligraphy on the Beautiful Names. It is certainly an act of self-discipline and dedication that could be easily described as worship.

The Prophet ﷺ has said that 'God is Beautiful and He loves Beauty.' So for me, writing his Names should be an act of beauty too. I've discovered harmony and balance through Arabic calligraphy and often I 'get lost in the work'. The feeling is like swimming in an ocean of His meanings, as if one is immersed in another world where the only thing at that particular moment is the inner journey towards the divine, and then art becomes discourse between the soul and spirit. Through art, you're able to open other doors of your being and experience more about the meanings of the 99 Names than just through thinking alone.

The mind should always be 'in peace'. One meaning of Islam is 'peace'. I used to try to be in a peaceful state of mind when I composed Islamic art, but now, I do Islamic art to help me be in a peaceful state! I see this is a blessing from God.

Q: When you work with a class on this kind of art, how do the pupils respond?

A: Pupils really love it! I think that they find it fascinating to learn letters in another language and use calligraphy in a new way.

In some secondary schools, students are able to express opinions and ask questions they've got in their minds regarding Muslims and the War on Terror. Many pupils are pleasantly surprised that Muslims can be artists too. And the fact that they enjoy doing Islamic art makes them appreciate religious life a little more. Teachers also love Arabic calligraphy. Many teachers have found this sort of art to be useful in introducing Islam as a topic and also in a purely Art lesson they've felt that all children can contribute as it is abstract. Pupils don't necessarily have to be great at copying.

They feel they've learnt a new skill. Most of all, they learn through fun. I think that as they are focused on writing the word 'Allah' they then form questions about what they are doing. For instance Who is Allah? Where is Allah? Why do people use different names for God? I get a lot of questions like this.

Interview your partner

- What sort of person is Razwan?
- What would you like to ask him?
- How do you think creativity and religion are connected?
- Can you find peace through artistic activity?
- Do you 'worship' in the kind of ways Razwan describes?
- What are your questions about God?

© 2008 RE Today Services
Permission is granted to photocopy this page for use in classroom activities in schools that have purchased this publication.

Activity 2 Sacred writing in Islam

Islamic calligraphy is a wonderful way of introducing children to how different faiths treat artefacts. As Islamic art is evoking the sacred, Muslims look after pieces of paper which have been used for religious calligraphy. Such work is not thrown away into the bin. We place the finished and unfinished work in a high place, a top shelf for example. If some work needs to be thrown away, it can be burnt, buried or carefully recycled. Teachers and pupils might like to follow the guidelines above when doing some of the tasks suggested.

I always try to use the word 'Allah'. I do this because I want children to engage in the fact that the notion of God is absolutely central in Islam. If children were just writing their names in Arabic then they would be doing Arabic rather than Islamic art. It's important to distinguish between the two.

And focusing on the Arabic word for God is also a brilliant springboard for further discussion. For instance, as 'Allah' is a generic name, it's not just Muslims who use that word. So what does that say about the Muslim belief regarding the nature of God? You could go further and use the calligraphy of the 99 Names of God. These beautiful names tell the believer how Islam speaks of Allah.

Arabic letters

Can you practise writing the letters in each shape?

Learning objectives		To do
In this work you will: • understand that there are different ways of writing Arabic letters • practise simple calligraphy yourself, using different media and colour to create effects. • compare and contrast ways of writing from different cultures.	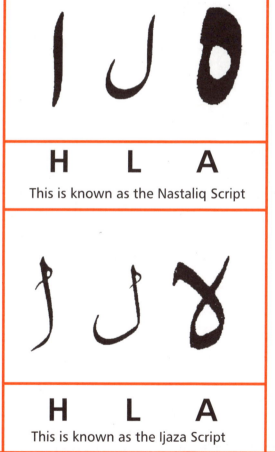 **H L A** This is known as the Nastaliq Script **H L A** This is known as the Ijaza Script	• Have a go at copying the letters. • With pastel or paint, try to recreate some of the letters. Use colours that you think are appropriate. You may want to use very strong bright colours, or you may want to make your design have pale or no colour at all. • Are some colours more suitable than others? Why? • Collect some examples of joined-up Arabic calligraphy. Are there some pieces that have more of an impact on you than others? Why? • How would you compare Arabic calligraphy with Chinese calligraphy? • What similarities do you see between the two different scripts?

Some more of the 99 Beautiful Names of Allah: The Eternal, He Who Pardons, The Provider, The Opener, The Hearer, The Hidden, The Raiser (of the dead).

© 2008 RE Today Services
Permission is granted to photocopy this page for use in classroom activities in schools that have purchased this publication.

REtoday
Services

Activity 3 The word 'Allah'

The letters 'a', 'l', 'l' and 'h' are used to write the word 'Allah' (read from right to left). Muslims believe that the word itself is sacred. There have been debates in Muslim history as to whether the Qur'an, being the divine word, is created and temporary or uncreated and eternal. Whatever view you may have, Muslims take great care to protect any surface where this word is written. (Note that the word Allah is Arabic, and hence Christian Arabs as well as other non-Muslim Arabs use the word 'Allah' for God.)

Nine different ways of writing the word Allah
(remember they are all read from right to left):

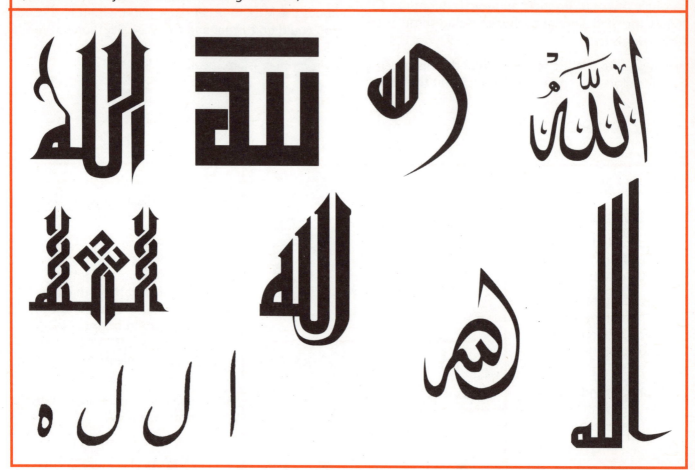

Learning objectives:

- to recognise motifs in Arabic script
- to recognise vital symbols of Islamic art
- to be able to read and write the word 'Allah'
- to think about the significance of the word and the script in Islam.

To do

- Can you make up some of your own ways of writing 'Allah'?
- You can use different shapes. You could try writing the word 'Allah' in triangles, squares, rectangles and more complex shapes such as the rhombus and hexagon. Elongate and shorten letters and join lines for greater artistic effects.
- The paper on which the word Allah is written is respected by Muslims and kept in a safe place, never thrown away in the bin, but disposed of carefully. Explain why this is important for Muslims.
- Just as you have different fonts in English, you have different ways of writing letters in Arabic. Can you try to find out how to write the word 'Allah' in the following Arabic scripts: Diwani/Maghrabi/Rihani/Tughra/Muhaqaq/Taj/Sumbuli?
- How would you describe the differences between each way of writing Allah on the next page?
- Which type would look better on the border? Why?
- Which script seems the easiest, and which the hardest? Why?

© 2008 RE Today Services
Permission is granted to photocopy this page for use in classroom activities in schools that have purchased this publication.

Examples of pupils' work from Activity 2

These can be seen in colour on the RE Today website (this term's password always in *REtoday* magazine).

Year 3 pupils made this calligraphic example with paint.

Spiritual calligraphy with paint from 10-year-olds

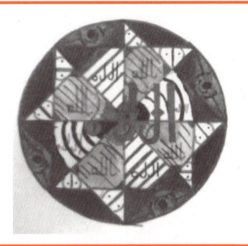

Year 5 pupils made this example with felt-tip pens.

The word 'Allah' is a suitable topic: a beautiful name for beautiful writing.

Design of a 14-year-old using a compass and calligraphy ink pens to produce the word Allah repeated many times.

High school pupils in Cumbria used ink made from walnut shells and sharpened sticks to do Arabic calligraphy. To add colour, pupils also used paint.

RE Today weblink:

www.retoday.org.uk

Further resources to support this activity are available to subscribers on the RE Today website.

© 2008 RE Today Services
Permission is granted to photocopy this page for use in classroom activities in schools that have purchased this publication.

Ten simple ways to mix more creativity into RE

This final section of the book provides a swift set of ideas that might enable you to introduce that creative element into a lesson without needing to spend your whole budget on fabric, glue and gold foil. The more creative RE classroom is as likely to emerge from these small-scale interventions as it is to be accomplished by a visiting orchestra. These ideas are sketched, but the best ideas are in your own head. Try some!

1. **Playdough** is a wonderful, reusable resource. You can buy 30 tiny pots – a class set – for less than £10. Looking at symbols of faith, pupils can make one for the religion they know most about, and one for a theme: remembrance, trust, faith or whatever. When you start work on life after death, ask pupils to mould something that might be found in heaven, then something that might be found in hell. Working on sanctity of life issues, ask pupils to mould a foetus, and then choose four emotional words that describe their feeling about the fact that they were once this small. Once you begin to use this for starters, you will not stop.

2. **Creativity in Hindu murti-making:** One artistic occupation for a talented Hindu is in making murtis or images of the gods and goddesses. These murtis are made of all sorts of materials from plastic to bronze, from painted clay to stone sculpture. While murtis are objects for devotion and worship, they also celebrate the human form and animal forms in a sensual and sensory way. When beginning a study of Hindu gods and goddesses, ask pupils to look at some murtis, and try to describe how they think the artefacts were made. Ask them to guess how long the maker took to create the murti. www.sacredsource.com is an interesting starting point for this exploration.

3. **Collage a concept** is an idea with a hundred uses in RE. All you need is a large box of magazines (donated Sunday supplements are perfect) and a nice tight brief for the pupils. Don't get them just to collage 'suffering'. Instead ask them to choose an appropriate single colour for the border, and incorporate physical, mental and spiritual suffering in the images the choose. Ask them to collage 'heaven and hell' with a line of grey in between them on a single sheet. In a unit on Christian belief, ask them to make a cross in the centre of a piece of A3, then collage into the four corners images of life, death, kindness and unkindness: they all relate to the gospel narratives of crucifixion in some ways.

4. **Sand mandalas in the Buddhist tradition:** To illustrate both mindfulness and impermanence, Buddhist monks sometimes create the most beautiful and detailed mandalas out of different coloured sands. It takes great mindfulness to get every grain just right. When they have been perfectly made, they are destroyed – tipped away, or dismantled. This illustrates the Buddhist idea that everything changes, nothing is permanent. Look at www.artnetwork.com/mandala/gallery for a visual feast on this theme. Pupils might consider whether throwing the mandala away at the end of the process is a good way to express belief in impermanence. Can pupils make an equivalent out of lentils, pasta, rice or some other disposable substance?

© 2008 RE Today Services
Permission is granted to photocopy this page for use in classroom activities in schools that have purchased this publication.